# Navigating

# the

# Female Universe

By
Mark Dobbs

Navigating the Female Universe

**Copyright © by Mark Dobbs**

All Rights Reserved

Mark Dobbs

# Table of Contents

Introduction

Chapter 1 – In the Beginning God Created Man and Then Woman to Ask Questions and Disobey Simple Rules

Chapter 2 – Women See Deeper Meanings

Chapter 3 – Sex Part I, the Un-evolved Male

Chapter 4 – Sex Part II, Evolving Male

Chapter 5 – Simple Creatures, Change Them All

Chapter 6 – Are We All Gay or Lesbian?

Chapter 7 – Look At Me!

Chapter 8 – The Point System

Chapter 9 – Asking for Directions or Any Help for that Matter

Chapter 10 – The Shopping Conundrum

Chapter 11 – A Simple Yes or No is All I Want

Chapter 12 – Beer Isn't a Food Group

Navigating the Female Universe

Chapter 13 – The FU Thinks Men Have a Hearing Problem and Perhaps a Little Vision Impairment Too

Chapter 14 – Compromise to Settlement

Chapter 15 – PMS Doesn't Stand for "Pissed at Men Syndrome"

Epilogue – For Women Only

Afterword

Glossary

Men's Self Help Test

All the Lessons – In the FU…

Mark Dobbs

# Introduction

Men, if your wife, fiancé, or girlfriend knows you're reading this she might expect that you're trying to evolve.

***Yeah right.*** Evolve into something you probably can't or won't become. But hey - Don't lose the moment… Let her believe. Can't hurt, can it? Might even be worth a few points later.

Look, your female partner has probably already read this guide or at least heard all about it. If she hasn't, you can bet she's going to read it after you're finished. She's going to know what you're doing, and most likely know more about what you're doing than you know yourself. She always knows what you're doing. Even when you think she doesn't have a clue about what you're doing – she does. She might not know at the exact moment you're doing something that you don't want her to know, but she's going to know. It's one of the unwritten and incontrovertible rules in the Female Universe.

So if you're really going to survive in the Female Universe you need to have at least a basic understanding of your relative position. Women take self-help surveys in every magazine they seem to read. They are constantly measuring themselves against other so-called "normal" women and, more importantly at this point, they even take quizzes that score YOU and your performance against some mythical "normal" man. So here's a guide and a chance for you to self assess. You owe yourself at least one tool that might help. Bottom line, a little knowledge might help you get around a bit easier in the Female Universe.

By the way, this is a "guide," not some academic, psycho-babble tome written by co-mingled PhD's trying to get tenured at a liberal arts university.

Mark Dobbs

***Here's what this guide is NOT.*** It isn't a strategy to fix an already destroyed marriage or long-term relationship or really messed up short term relationship for that matter. It is not a substitute for professional counseling. It is not a coffee table book for Dr. Phil, Jerry Springer or Ellen DeGeneres. It definitely isn't intended to be too serious. It is not a rebuttal for women's lib. For what it's worth, women didn't need men's permission or help to be liberated anyway. The whole liberation movement was a male response to females making a very carefully conceived move as part of the greater Female Universe plan. And finally, this guide will not make women want to regain the Jackie Kennedy or June Cleaver image of the perfect woman in nylons and high heels waiting at home in her perfectly manicured and coifed form for her big stud husband to come home, later than expected, for a home cooked supper. Get over it. There isn't a book that can create that.

Navigating the Female Universe

***Here's what this guide IS***. It is a guide that may help some of you pick up after yourself (assuming you're a slob already) for a day or two to try to "make points". There may be one or two men ready to make some changes. Reading this might encourage them to look for an academic tome on the subject or to seek professional counseling. This is a formal recognition that women really do run the universe. Some guys will argue about this… ***with other guys.*** They won't argue it with women. It is an attention getter. Your wife or girl friend might look at you differently. It will be your job to figure out the look. It could be good. Let's hope for good. This guide is mostly a light hearted look at the Female Universe from a common man's perspective and the relative effect of men's behaviors in the Female Universe.

# Chapter 1

# In the Beginning God Created Man and Then a Woman to Ask Questions and Disobey Simple Rules

The Female Universe (or "FU" from here on) is a truly complex concept. No matter what you might otherwise think, even if you're a dyed-in-the-wool male chauvinist, you need to relent and understand that women **DO** control the known universe. Look, in the beginning God created Man and then, for many reasons, God also created Woman (this means many reasons NOT related to having sex – most men have a single, simple focus which will be unraveled later in the book).

Assuming normal developmental rules for creating, or prototyping a new product – the first prototype of any new creation is usually simpler and cruder. The second prototype generally has fewer flaws and is less crude than its predecessor. Therefore, it is simple deductive reasoning to assume that the second person God created, the Female, may have been considered an "improved" model. This book acknowledges that most guys want to be successful in their environment and that the way to do that to some degree is to learn how to be creative and agile in that environment. It doesn't matter if the environment is work or sports or even romance – a few simple tools might give smart men a bit of an edge.

Women have made their way into all facets of what men wanted to believe was male dominated life and have been actively competing with guys and each other for years. They are clearly and continually shattering the so-called "glass ceiling" which post-Industrial Age women built. Yes, women built it. Men just perpetuated the myth.

## Mark Dobbs

Until the human race evolved technically, culturally and financially to the point it is today – men seemed to be at the center of the business, military and political worlds. Men were left to believe that **THEY** built nearly everything. Men would puff out their chests and pat each other on the back as they accomplished what seemed to be incomprehensible feats. Women would ration out kisses and hugs to congratulate their business, military or political warrior and feasts would be prepared where friends and children would be told stories about how their fathers, uncles, grandfathers, etcetera made things possible to usher in some new era of whatever.

In bygone times, most men believed that women were supposed to be at home taking care of the household. They raised the children and tended to all sorts of family matters. It was their "place."

Did you ever think that perhaps women purposely let the men do the back breaking labor from daylight to dark everyday building homes, farms, towns, roads, waterways, and so on? Men died young from war, disease and literally the back-breaking work that it took to get most of the world into the technologically advanced environment many of us currently enjoy. Women chose to stay sheltered, warm and clean to the extent technology and finances allowed.

Every man seems to want to believe the notion that women are the "fairer" or "weaker" sex. That brawn is somehow superior as sexes go. Okay, so men are stronger generally. Today, women can lift or carry anything men can by using machines or steroids or simply doing what most men won't do – they ask for help. Even if society collapsed and technology failed all together, women could survive without men. Women can learn to hunt and fish as well as, if not better than, many men in modern life who have never fished or hunted. In addition to all that, women generally seem to collaborate better than men and appear more adept at communal living where survival has the best chance and requires the most cooperation.

So what? Think about this – women don't really need men in today's technologically improved world. Even making babies can be done by artificial means. After all, with just a little work, women could store enough "donated" sperm from willing males to last for millennia.

The female is clearly the most flexible human form. They can make life, nourish it inside and outside the womb, nurture and educate the newborn through adolescence and into adulthood without a man. If that weren't enough, women generally live longer and stay mentally sharper for much longer than most men. Just ask any actuarial at a major life insurance company for the statistics.

By the way, the "world-wide-web"… it was alive and working reasonably well beginning shortly after the human race learned to communicate and it was women who made it work most effectively. In the earliest days, women found ways to send messages and hold meetings when the men were out doing "men's work". There was a code, still is for the most part, that only women could decipher. Men just called it gossip and ignored what they didn't understand.

Women would decide where towns, schools, stores, roads and the like needed to be built by having multiple conversation via the gossip channels and then would have very carefully planned conversations with their men. These conversations usually happened at the dinner table or just before sex. Women have always known that they only had a man's real attention when there was a meal in front of him or sex was beckoning. Usually, after either of these the men would fall asleep and any attention was lost until the next meal or sexual opportunity.

The day after these carefully contrived informal dining room or bedroom meetings the men would then share ***"their"*** newly found creative idea or ideas with the rest of the men and the next thing you know, interstate highways connected cities, states and countries. Not to mention ideas for developing electricity, splitting the atom, heart surgery and television. Women, it would seem, even coined the expression, "behind every good man, there's a woman."

Of course, not every notion will fit every theory. Take Madam Curie for example. Like so many other great women in history, it would appear that she didn't have a man in her life that could fully understand her amazing ideas – so she had to do most of the work herself. Or maybe, occasionally, the woman was just a bit rebellious in the earlier days and chose to break out of the common FU plan.

The FU is everywhere. You can't escape from it or to it. But as technology advances and more women continue breaking through higher and tougher "glass ceilings" they seem to be moving further away from the "old" FU ways. New, technologically superior FU tools are being developed and young females are being trained in the "new" ways without even knowing they are part of something as old as history itself.

Look around you. Social networking is all the rage. Computers and cell phones make the world-wide-web in the modern FU extremely fast and incredibly broad. Even men believe that there's some socially undeniable benefit to telling every little detail of their daily life on various electronic social networking sites. Men and kids are more and more willing to share detailed accountings of their travels and activities with anyone willing to befriend them. Did you ever think that perhaps it's just part of an FU tactic of ongoing monitoring?

Your real friends, the close ones that you trust, know where you are and what you're doing without logging in to your social page. In fact, they're probably with you for the most part. The only people gaining anything from your courageous postings are the women who carefully decipher your intricate offerings.

In the FU, every minute of your behavior is closely accounted. Minutes that are not specifically accounted for are those when you are under direct observation. If your story on a web-site is the least bit out of sync with any other record or observation by the FU then you're going to have a reckoning. It's inescapable. Someone in the FU will ultimately report the discrepancy in your pattern of activity. The really scary part is that what women need to share with the rest of the FU is shared nearly instantaneously to every pin prick of light on the planet where technology is available.

With great advances in technology come great changes in culture and wider acceptance of the things the FU wants you to believe are popular, fun and needed. Computer aided match makers, social networks, IM, chatting, tweeting, tagging and location tracking software attached to photos and text mails give the FU more info than the CIA and KGB had during the peak of the Cold War. If you text or send a photo to a friend, who in turn sends it to his wife or girlfriend for some reason, your wife will know where you are at almost the moment you've hit the send button.

So if you're texting from the race track or your favorite fishing hole then don't say you're somewhere else. She will know, she probably already knows, she always knows. If you only get one thing from this guide – know this: Truth is your best tool for a good defense.

-------------------------------------------------

***<u>First lesson</u>:** An un-evolved man is, and always will be an unarmed man in the FU.*

## Chapter 2

## Women See Deeper Meanings in Most Things and What You See Isn't What You Always Get!

This is the first concept you need to understand clearly before moving to more complex notions. Simple premise don't you think? Yet most men don't seem to understand this notion. Most women, however, understand this very clearly.

In the FU things are never simple or straight forward. Many women would have you believe that everything, especially the concepts that are specifically presented as *simple*, have a deeper and more complicated core.

It's not their fault that they think this way.

Take a look at an early example from human history. Stone Age man would create a useful tool.

## Navigating the Female Universe

Something very simple… a sharpened rock perhaps. By the time he finished showing other men and women all of the things he could do with this simple tool and explained a little about how it could be used for many things, he had made himself sound like a folk hero and had inadvertently made the tool sound incredibly complicated.

First of all, the man was probably just messing around with some rocks, probably flint, and when the flint started chipping in an interesting way it kept the man occupied and out of the woman's way for hours. Once the rock was adequately chipped and chiseled, this early man probably cut his hand accidentally on the new tool and ***voila*** a cutting tool was invented.

He would delight in the ease and simplicity of using the tool. He could gut a fish or skin a rabbit with a few easy movements. Suddenly, he looked like a skilled craftsman. He was no longer tearing at a hide with a broken shell or stick, no longer having to rip at dead animal flesh with his teeth. In fact, he was somehow more civilized than he had been just a few hours before.

As he demonstrated the new tool, a sharpened rock remember, the tool took on an amazing and wonderful life of its own. The man would embellish on how he skillfully chipped and chiseled its edge and then tested his progress until it was perfectly sharp and could perform the task he required. He ***had*** to embellish. He couldn't admit that he was just "playing" and then cut himself.

Other men saw the tool, ignored the explanation and any directions, and intuitively saw the usefulness as "a cutting tool".

Women became caught up in the multiple possible uses and various nuances perceived in the uses. Before long, a woman would ask the inventor for a simple instruction manual so that she and other women would be able to enjoy the many options the tool offered. Cave drawings were almost always simple instruction manuals left by men to document their discoveries and to train others.

Children would try to mimic the story of how the new tool had been invented. They would pick up rocks and smack them together with nothing to show except for bruised fingers. They would run to their mothers crying. The mother, not knowing anything about the process to make the tool themselves would explain how it was too complicated for children and that only a skillful craftsman such as their father could make the tool.

Of course the people of that day didn't know they needed the new tool until they actually saw it being artfully manipulated and working. Then everyone had to have one. Since the actual material and process for creating the tool was only known to one man, he probably became rich and famous. Well, as rich and famous as you could be back in the day of stone tools. The point is – it was a simple creation, created by a simple man. It was invented by accident. It intuitively cut stuff. Simple…

We still do the same thing today. A new tool gets invented and marketed as the miracle of miracles. The tool is guaranteed to save hours of work every week and suddenly, even though no one ever heard of it before, everyone needs one. And then you hear the pitch man - "This sharpened stone minces, it slices, it dices and chops. You can cut hair or hide. This product does it all and if you act now you can pay one low price and you'll get two of these amazing new indestructible tools that are safe to use over and over again without dulling or rusting! No household should be without one."

Really? Slices and dices? Come on - IT CUTS STUFF!

Men made a simple tool sound and behave as something much more complicated than it really was to perpetuate their self importance and impress women. After eons of this behavior, women learned that nearly everything had a deeper, richer and more complicated core. Here's the twist… they were right, almost everything was and ***IS*** more complicated.

So, where were we? Oh yes – Women, of course, acted appropriately impressed with the man's invention and the overly embellished explanation. However, women immediately saw the expanding and more complicated reality of the sharp cutting stone. It ***didn't*** just cut stuff! It was power!

Early woman understood the cutting stone could logically provide wealth and status. It wasn't just a tool to be used in the rough ways man described. It could be used for more intricate things as well.

Soon, women without the tool were jealous of those who had the tool. If they didn't have the ability to obtain a tool of their own through the normal barter method, then they would convince their man to steal one. Perhaps another man would be killed in the process of stealing. The horrific deeds would lead to the creation of tribunals, laws, courts, governments and all forms of complicated things would be born as a result of a simple invention.

Okay, it's a stretch. The need for governance probably wasn't born from a single rock tool. But you should get the idea by now. In the FU the simplest of things will have multiple, sometimes complex meanings and most of the time what women want you to see is NOT the only thing you're going to get. Yes, it has been going on since the caveman – but the FU made it work effectively. Cosmetics, girdles, nylons, hair color and the like… you'll see what women want you to see *and* you'll very likely get more than you expected. Maybe good, maybe bad – certainly more than you expected.

--------------------------------------------------

***Second lesson:** In the FU, women generally see deeper meanings in everything and what men see isn't always what they get!*

# Chapter 3

## Sex Part I, the Un-evolved Male

Oh sure, it starts out simple enough. A woman finds you appealing for some reason. Perhaps she likes your face, your physique, your car, or your shoes… who knows? Either way, you think she wants you. You like the attention AND she's sexually appealing to you. Yes, sexually appealing. We are, after all, still animals in many ways. Perpetuating the species is part of the survival instinct.

The more evolved men reading this may cringe at this and swear that they are somehow attracted to the woman's mind and other formidable attributes. Heaven forbid they should be seen as animals and admit that there is a simple *sexual* attraction. The FU sees the partially evolved man is trying to be accepting of women's desire to be attractive for more than just sexual reasons. He will be rewarded by women and misunderstood by less evolved men.

Once the selection is made there will be the normal testing period. We call it dating, going out, or being exclusive. It used to be courting or pitching woo. Whatever you call it, it's still the same thing – ***it's a TEST!***

Sure, the male wants to get through the test successfully. But honestly, in the earliest meetings the man usually only has one objective – to have sex. Yes, almost every guy secretly and sinfully wants to score with a woman he finds sexually appealing. In fact, the less evolved man would always like to have sex on a first date. For many men this is a true sign of his evolved "masculinity". If he can win a women's sexual favor on the first date then he feels extra special or successful somehow. This perceived "victory" as it were, has caused many ill rumors and fights from high school through adulthood. Puny little geeks all the way to football heroes have been guilty of saying they were "victorious" when in fact they were not. Men even perpetuated a sliding scale scoring system many years ago. Some guys would get to "first base" on the first date, while others might "hit a homerun".

Sex, not emotional fulfillment, is still the singular reward for most men. In fact, if a man can't find someone he considers really sexy or "hot" to have sex with, then he may settle for "not bad" and finally, if all else fails; he may settle for a woman he finds less than appealing (or ugly) as long as the promise of sex is still a reward. What most guys fail to understand is that women, most of them, want emotional fulfillment first. Women, particularly mature women in the FU, have to have emotional fulfillment before the sex act is satisfying to them.

In the FU the rules are very complex concerning the courting behavior. There is almost never the promise of sex. Well, almost never – there are some exceptions if you know what to look for.

Women can use any courting ritual they choose and can change their rules without any notice. Women control how and when the sexual reward may be distributed. Modern man must be very observant and remain extremely flexible.

Consider all the possibilities and combinations of female behavior. They can be categorized for ease of explanation. The list below is not all inclusive as there can be thousands of categories. The evolved man needs to at least be able to recognize some of the possibilities and once he recognizes a category or combination of categories, he should be able to navigate the FU a bit better.

Here are some possible categories:

The Pro – These aren't just streetwalking lower life forms trying to earn money to pay for their next drug fix. Some aren't recognizable at all. This category includes women who exchange sex for favors. Sometimes the favors are work related or favors for social status and recognition. This is a dangerous category no matter who you are and should be avoided unless you happen to really be sexually attracted to the woman and have nothing to lose except your immortal soul of course.

The cougar – A category that seems to have made a resurgence in the last few years although it is as old as time itself. A cougar is usually considered an older woman who is looking for a younger man. The man, regardless of age, wants sex and wants to be considered sexually appealing to the woman. The woman is recapturing the feeling of her youth by being sexually appealing to a younger man. It's a win-win… sort of…

The lesbian – There are multiple subcategories. Some are feminine, some are masculine, some are somewhere in between. What's important is that you save yourself from the humiliation of being rejected. You may try out your smoothest opening line only to have it lost on a woman who believes you're already an extinct species in the FU. This category should generally be avoided. If you happen to find a woman who is experimenting as a hetero because she hasn't fully committed to her homosexual life or perhaps she has been recently rejected by her female lover, it is generally recommended that you have sex and enjoy the moment – but don't get attached.

The transvestite – This is not a woman. Therefore, no matter what the hormones, clothes and surgeries have done this is not a true member of the FU. This is a man trying to become an accepted member of the FU. Some members of the FU will accept the changeling as one of their own. There is no birth right to full entitlement within the FU and some of these people will fail to assimilate. You may be fooled and have sex with one of these. If you didn't know what it was when it happened then just take a deep breath and get your HIV test and be happy if the sex was somehow good for you.

The cheating wife – This is a scary category for a man looking to "score" on a first date. It will likely be riddled with difficulty; you could end up dead or in jail. Still, the sex will probably be extremely good. Remember, most cheating women are looking for one or two things. Some are looking for sexual excitement because they are bored at home. Others are looking for emotional excitement because they are bored at home. Some are looking for both. Emotionally challenged cheating wives can cause confusion and should be avoided.

The independent professional – These women are generally looking for companionship and sex. Not necessarily in that order. Many of these women are secure in their professional lives and consider themselves to be emotionally under control. They know that they are in the higher order of the FU and that they really don't need men. Men are like an item on the menu and these women expect that they can order him like they would order caviar or wine. Men who choose this path should be prepared to be discarded like yesterday's technology.

The SadFab's – This is a woman who is *S*ingle *A*nd *D*esperate *F*or *A* *B*aby. They really do have their own acronym. She is running from her biological clock. She needs sperm. Her goal is simple as long as she isn't looking for a lifelong companion. She wants a man, preferably a man that appears to have the physical and mental attributes that make her believe that her offspring will be physically capable and intellectually successful. If she is looking for a life mate then all the other emotional issues will come into play, however, the driving factor will still be getting the best looking and smartest sperm provider she can find.

The emotionally needy – This is an interesting category. Some men still believe they should be problem solvers and see an emotionally needy woman as something they can "fix". The reality is that the emotionally needy woman really only wants someone to listen to them. Men shouldn't try to fix anything. Just listen or at least act like you're sincerely interested and that you're listening. Don't talk, don't offer advice, just nod. Nod up and down to show agreement and nod sideways when you hear something that is apparently devastating, demeaning, or sad. Nodding up and down may be interpreted as showing understanding and sideways shows empathy. These are positive feedback mechanisms and using them appropriately will be rewarded. *(Note: **The nodding technique described here is extremely valuable and may be employed at other times. Learn it and be prepared to put it to good use when needed!**)*

The nymphomaniac – Yes, these women really exist in the FU. If you find one and she wants you, gird your loins! She will likely wear you out before you could possibly wear her out. She is a sexual predator in the FU and will go through average men with almost no compunction and zero emotional investment. You aren't special and she will make you realize this in a hurry. Remember basic human physiology… a woman can perform sexually repetitively and frequently and without much recuperative time. Guys, even young guys, need recuperation between events. You will end up no better than an expended, limp and discarded toy.

The ugly women – Don't be misled, the FU allows all types of women to be active members. These women are usually not threatening and are generally tucked into many other categories. These women have sexual needs and often find themselves rejected in social settings. Men can and do take advantage of this category for quick sex. Almost everyone knows the "categories" of ugly. They apply to men equally… but since this guide is for men, this is about women for now. Generically these categories are the "one bagger", "two bagger", and "Coyote ugly. If you aren't familiar with these terms then look them up in the glossary at the back of the book.

There are still untold numbers of other categories. Every man should simply acknowledge that he now understands that there are different requirements depending on the woman. The FU is not easy and one size or type will not always fit. Remember, be flexible. Here are a few other categories to ponder on your own:

-The model, TV/movie star, singer, etc., basically the rich and famous;

-The cheerleader;

-The prom queen;

-The geek;

-The high school sweetheart;

-The college sweetheart;

-The sorority girl;

Navigating the Female Universe

-The woman who owns her own fishing boat, hunting lodge that looks like a cheerleader and loves to cook, clean and have sex in morning. There has to be at least one in the FU – right?

Finally, combinations of categories are very real and exceedingly complex. For example: If the SadFab woman and independent professional categories merged, you might see a very beautiful professional woman who really feels her biological clock ticking away; she will be smart and probably has the money and means to raise a very happy and healthy baby on her own – all she needs is sperm. This woman busted the glass ceiling easily and she knows her most efficient way to get a biologically superior baby is to get professionally screened and safe sperm from a high end sperm bank. Dating can be seen as inefficient and dangerous to this woman. You aren't going to just "get lucky". This woman is a fully evolved member of the FU and knows that she doesn't need men for anything.

Stay focused! You *can* navigate the FU for sex. It already takes a lot of work right? You might make it more meaningful and improve your success rate with a little hard work. Failure equates to loneliness – so what have you got to lose, besides your immortal soul?

---

***Third lesson:*** *In the FU, nodding appropriately is a key communication tool for men. Keep the conversation focused on the woman.*

# Chapter 4

## Sex Part II, Evolving Male

Guys, this next concept may be hard for many of you to grasp.

Sex, it seems, isn't just for men.

Most women thoroughly enjoy sexual satisfaction. So, surviving and navigating the FU depends on your ability to **satisfy the woman**. Remember, the FU has the upper hand and controls the known universe. After you think that you've figured out the selection process and a woman has allowed you to begin the courting process you will discover that your urgent sexual needs may not be seen as urgent as you might like.

Women, with very few exceptions, want an emotional entanglement. For women, generally, there needs to be a positive exchange of glances and conversation and the appearance of, or promise of, a mutually beneficial relationship. These glances, conversations and other offerings such as flowers, dinner, and gifts may be considered parts of the action known as romance. Romance is one of the higher pre-sexual stages in developing the relationship, which ***might*** lead to sex.

That's right… relationship. In the FU the relationship is king! Or queen? Whatever…

As hard as it is (figure of speech) you must put aside thoughts of immediate sex and try to think about being as engaging as possible for the woman. In the previous chapter we clearly realized that the unrestrained male would be happy with sex, for any reason, with practically any woman as long as it happened at or about the time the man wanted it. The reality… it doesn't happen like that usually. There is good news though.

Navigating the Female Universe

It seems that the more engaging you become to women, the easier it will be for you to reap the rewards. To become engaging, the man must prepare, practice and put himself in the right locations to improve his chances for success.

When men hunt, let's say hunt ducks, they have learned that there are certain behaviors that will improve their chances for a successful hunt. Most of what they have learned came from observing other successful duck hunters. They also read duck hunting books and magazines and watch "self-help" or "how-to" instructional videos about duck hunting. These guys literally immerse themselves into understanding their quarry.

The best duck hunters also practice the various skills it takes to hunt ducks. Some will go to a sporting clays or skeet range to practice shooting their shotguns. Duck hunters will also spend time practicing duck calls so that they can imitate either the male or female duck sounds or various sounds that signal feeding or roosting behaviors.

Duck hunters may spend hours preparing their duck hunting apparel to be sure they gain every conceivable advantage to blend in with their environment as to not spook the ducks. Finally, the duck hunter will prepare the hunting location or pay someone; a guide perhaps, to make sure the place to hunt will be perfectly setup for duck hunting.

After careful planning and hard work it is clearly understood that the duck hunter *expects* to have a very productive hunt and if the ducks are cooperating – he will be highly successful. His success will be attributed to his superior preparation.

From the simple example of duck hunting you can and should have learned the basic tools you will need to move deftly in the FU as an evolved and sexually maturing man. Here are the steps again:

1. Choose your target.

Navigating the Female Universe

2. Find the best locations.

3. Observe successful men's behaviors and try to emulate.

4. Read "self-help" guides. For men this means reading certain women's magazines and taking the tests that women usually take related to rating their husband, boyfriend, or lover. (Don't worry, most of them are the same, just choose one or two.)

5. Practice your communication skills by engaging women in conversations at work or some other non-dating, stress free, safe environment.

6. Improve your wardrobe.

There you are. Simple! Only six steps in the process.

Steps one through three are fairly straight forward and most of you will understand them. Choosing your target simply means that you need to decide what general category of woman you find appealing. Perhaps a western cowgirl or big city lawyer, it's really your choice. Preparation and planning will help you reach your target. After you decide on a target, go to where they are most likely to be found in social settings. These settings can range from libraries, churches, honkytonks, private country clubs and so on. Observe how the apparently successful male behaves in the social environment that you've chosen. If you consider yourself the successful male in this chosen environment, then skip to the next step.

Step four may be considered a bit bizarre. It is not the intent of this guide to encourage you to read these women's magazines from front cover to back. If you do, and you talk about it with another man, you may be looked at as if you were bordering on gay behavior. Also, don't start reading the magazine in the super market checkout line or in the lounge at your favorite book monger's shop.

Navigating the Female Universe

Okay, you've chosen a magazine. For this guide we'll call the magazine Pink Book Ladies World.

If you scan through your copy of Pink Book you will undoubtedly find at least one, if not several, personality or self help quizzes. There are three types generically:

a. Women's self exploration of psyche composed of many possible variants.
b. Women's self exploration of physical conditions.
c. Women's search to understand men.

Start with the quizzes involving women trying to evaluate their men. Women have been evaluating and grading men for eons. You, or someone you know has been sliced, diced and pureed through the grading of simple quizzes like you will see in these magazines.

## Mark Dobbs

Oh sure... they were developed by some white haired, psychologist, psychiatrist, anthropologist or, better yet – a self professed guru of male patterned behaviors. It doesn't matter what you think about the little exam yourself. But you better understand what they do and how they can affect your life.

Each of these tests will give women the belief that their man doesn't measure up to the so-called ideal man. He could be close to ideal if the wife grades him generously, but generally all men fall short of ideal.

The definition of the ideal man is transitional at best. Perhaps one test rates the ideal man as a mixture of Genghis Kahn, Gandhi, Einstein, Fabio, Errol Flynn or Rock Hudson (think about it), and a touch of bad boy rock star. Another test will have a different target.

You will need to review several.

Navigating the Female Universe

What you should gain from these reviews is that women have many different beliefs about men and their behavior. Knowing what the perceptions might be will help you navigate a bit better. You will learn how subtleties can make enormous improvements in your image. For example: Having a picture of your puppy in your wallet makes you warm and sensitive. Just make sure the picture isn't next to the one with the dog all grown up with a dead duck in its mouth.

This little bit of knowledge comes with a warning – Never get comfortable, women's perceptions of the ideal man change constantly.

Steps five and six should be done together. As you improve your wardrobe you will find a bit more self-confidence and this will make you a bit more comfortable engaging in conversations with women in safe environments. Conversation is easier than it sounds. For the most part YOU don't really need to talk.

As it turns out - being a great listener will make you the favored partner for good conversation. Women really want someone who actively listens. If you're asked a question, feel free to answer. Don't dumb it down… huge mistake! Women will ask for explanations where or when needed. Most importantly, know when to shut-up. Don't go on and on about the answer. ***Get the conversation back to the woman.***

You are now engaging in a relationship. You are relating to the woman on an intellectual and emotional plane as it were.

If this stage is successful it may lead to romance. Romance may lead to sex. If the relationship stage is unsuccessful you can usually count out the chance of having sex. Come on, no one said this was easy.

If you fail the first time after step six, then repeat the steps carefully and pay more attention to the kinds of reactions you get from the women. It is also possible that you may have chosen the wrong target for your ability. If you fail again after step six then you may need to lower your standards.

-------------------------------------------------

***Fourth lesson**: In the FU, successful sexual coupling means engaging in relationships and romance. Evolving men can have reasonably successful relationships with women assuming they are willing to work and understand what's expected from them.*

# Chapter 5

## Simple Creatures, Change them All

The first hint indicating that you need help navigating the FU is when a woman, any woman, begins trying to change you or your behaviors.

Men are basically simple creatures, what you see - really is what you get. Quite frankly, men don't usually do a very good job at hiding their less-than-stellar habits. Generally, a woman can see a dirty, mislaid sock across the length of a house. But for some reason, during the courting process, she can ignore even the most vulgar behaviors displayed by "her man" depending on how insecure she might be about her own ability to attract a partner. The needier a woman is to have a partner and the more insecure she is about getting one – the more she is willing to overlook.

Navigating the Female Universe

What men need to understand about this practice is a bit more complex.

Women may overlook your vulgar, unsophisticated and disgusting behaviors to get through the romance, relationship building and commitment phases. In fact, most women could tell by your laundry, apartment, house and car that you were a slob but it may not have detracted them from getting to the end goal of ***commitment***. Somehow, commitment gives the woman in the FU a license to begin changing the man and the power to try.

You probably weren't intentionally misleading the woman. You never hid your untoward behavior. In fact, you may have even had lengthy conversations about neatness, laundry and the like. The woman may have even offered to save you from yourself and give you a hand with your little "insignificant" issues. You agreed eagerly of course, because you still had your eye on the reward… SEX! You would have said almost anything depending on how great your hormonally driven need may have been at that moment. Now you find yourself in need of help.

First of all, don't blame the woman…

In the FU, there is a tremendous investment by women throughout the world to monitor men and modify them in whole or in part. Every change successfully manipulated is one more small victory in the woman's evolution of man. This isn't war, but sometimes you will feel like it is.

The deeper your commitment to the woman, the greater the likelihood that you will undergo many attempts by her to modify your behavior. It will start subtly enough and then begin a sudden ramping-up as she wins the smaller battles. Here are some of the most common things she will likely make you consider:

1. Putting the toilet seat back down.

Navigating the Female Universe

2. Picking up your dirty underwear and putting them in a hamper or similar device.

3. Not belching or farting, in public – which means anywhere she can hear you or smell you. This may include your garage, basement, backyard and probably the neighborhood.

4. Eating at the dinner table instead of in front of the TV, unless it was her idea to eat in front of the TV. It won't be a ball game – it will probably be "Dancing with Rich and Famous" or something similar.

There will be dozens more of these change topics… It's an unwritten part of the rules in the FU. If you want to share in the commitment that you've apparently already agreed to then you may consider capitulating on some of the earliest things the woman asks. Your willingness to show that you are adaptable will win you some early ***points*** and a little leverage later. If you need a little motivation to continue this chapter you may want to skip ahead to the chapter concerning the ***Point System***. Points can be good if properly employed.

There appears to be a FU male change theorem which clearly states: "A woman who has been given a commitment by a man has the right to attempt to change him and to make him behave more like the woman." It is clearly somewhere in the fine print of the promise you made... it must be... otherwise why would every woman expect that she has this right?

In the "for what it's worth" category – there are some religious sects where men have created laws to prevent women from having the right to attempt changing the man's behavior. Don't think that joining one of these religions will free you. There are already too many women in various "human rights" organizations attempting to infiltrate and change the laws which bind these women. It really is only a matter of time before the FU will have the upper hand in every corner of the increasingly shrinking world.

---

***Fifth lesson***: *In the FU, women rarely believe the man is fine "as is." They believe there is always room for improvement. The kicker - your willingness to accept that you probably have faults and your willingness to change those things that can be changed will lead to your success in navigating in the FU.*

# Chapter 6

## Are We All Gay or Lesbian?

Don't let the title fool you. This chapter isn't about sex – it's a continuing examination of "relationships." So from that stand point at least… in the FU, all women are already Lesbians and men are mostly Gay!

It's true! Women want to be surrounded by other women. Okay, maybe not always Lesbians – but they definitely prefer the company of other women when they are ready to "relate." They like sharing feelings and getting support from empathetic members of their own gender. Many are members of bridge clubs, golf or tennis teams, quilting groups, lunch groups, gourmet cooking clubs and numerous other female only conclaves.

They share a common interest and develop trusting bonds with other women who enjoy the same type of relationship and can feel comfortable where womanly things are concerned. Sure, men try to join some of these groups. Some are even successful – generally the very effeminate ones who don't feel comfortable at the hunting lodge, men's only club, poker table or pool hall.

Likewise, men want to be around other men doing manly things and sharing their experiences with like minded men. Most guys, prior to andropause (glossary time), really haven't grown up emotionally very much since adolescence so there's still a need to "hang with the boys".

When guys get together they don't usually talk about emotional issues or health problems or recipes, children or their parents. They talk about work, cars, money, hobbies and anything worth bragging about. They don't talk about wives unless someone has a real ugly relationship or divorce coming. Then, the rest of the group may tolerate some talk about wives.

Guys with good to better than average relationships with a woman generally don't discuss their situations. Mainly because other guys don't want to hear the details – especially if these other guys have relationships that aren't at least at the "good" level yet. Rarely do you ever hear a man with other men bragging about his relationship. He may brag about his wife's cooking or good looks and, on occasion, about her job. But not about his relationship.

Talking about relationship stuff is just not a comfortable topic for men. Even talking about their relationship with their woman usually only involves a couple of things. First, and usually foremost – "sex." Secondly, and only because the man suspects that he is somehow in trouble – the conversation will start with him saying: "What did I do wrong?" This comes from man's two basic emotional needs. One is for "approval" and the other is the "look-at-me" complex. Both of these will be discussed in the next chapter.

Navigating the Female Universe

What does all this mean when it comes to navigating the FU?

Simple! Men and women need to accept that there are some differences in the physical and psychological makeup of our species and get on with life. Specifically:

- Men need to understand that women have a basic natural need to talk about relationships, and thousands of other things for that matter. Women are comfortable talking with other women and for some reason they believe that they should be able to do the same with "their" man. They aren't ***wrong*** about wanting to be able to relate with their man (in the FU – ***women may not always be right, but they're never wrong)***.
- Women need to understand that men generally don't want to talk about relationships until it's too late or they are forced to by court ordered counseling.

- Men need to be open to the fact that women want "their" man to talk honestly and openly with them but that honesty can have precipitous results. Warning - honesty has a relative relevance and must be used appropriately. Explore your options to the simple question, "Does this outfit make me look fat?" Remember - honesty has relative relevance, especially when the security of your relationship is at risk.
- Women should understand that men don't generally have a relationship problem just because they don't want to talk about the relationship – men aren't generally that "deep."
- Men should acknowledge that women have a need to discuss their relationships and, therefore, men are encouraged to adopt the "nod" approach discussed in chapter two. If you are pressed for conversation where a

## Navigating the Female Universe

simple nod won't work just remember the following phrases:

- I think you're the most beautiful woman I know.
- Of course I love you.
- You're the most important woman in my life.
- I'll try to do better. (Note: use this sparingly, and you had better be listening and taking notes so you'll know what you're supposed to do better. Failure to at least attempt to do whatever it is better will be grounds for retribution.)
- Women need to clearly understand men's basic emotional needs can be reduced and described as the "look-at-me" and "approval" concepts.
- Both sexes need to acknowledge that we should never, never try to talk about relationships when either or both parties have

been drinking or are engaged in foreplay or sex or are in public where anyone else can hear or any combination of these. Most importantly – never ask a question where you may get an answer that you already know you can't handle emotionally.

---

***Sixth lesson:** In the FU, an evolved man is able to understand that communicating about relationships is important – to the woman.*

# Chapter 7

## Look at Me!

You've heard the old joke:

First guy: "What's the last thing you hear before a Redneck dies?"

Second guy: "I don't know. What's the last thing you hear before a Redneck dies?"

First guy: "Hey Bubba! Watch this!"

Think about this for a minute… Every guy you've known from your earliest memory has, at one time or another, hollered for you or someone else or a bunch of people to "Watch this!" Boys, and many men, need to be seen! It's as if we're going to do something that's never been seen before and that what we're about to do may never be repeated and it can't go unnoticed!

## Mark Dobbs

Women in the FU, particularly mothers, understand this phenomenon. Children, boys and girls, are almost constantly haranguing their mothers and fathers (if they're around), with the phrase "watch me, watch me."

Somewhere along the way, most girls tend to grow out of the need to "show off". Boys, on the other hand, keep seeking an audience and watching closely for someone's nod of approval.

This constant need for approval doesn't diminish with time. As long as a man has enough testosterone to cause him to have an active ego he will seek attention for anything he considers an accomplishment. The list of things that can be considered accomplishments has no known end; therefore, men's need for approval is likewise never ending…

By the way, and for the record, getting approval isn't the same thing as getting permission.

## Navigating the Female Universe

Approval is more basic. It is as simple as a gesture from someone showing satisfaction for an act or giving a favorable opinion about the act. Verbal examples of someone showing satisfaction or giving a favorable opinion could include: "That's nice honey." "Good job!" "At least you didn't hurt yourself." "Were you sober when that happened?"

The FU understands this basic need much better than the men who continue seeking the approval but most women don't know how to make the most out this behavior. For men, believe it or not this is one of the greatest displays of emotional need that we can exhibit. Here's how that can work…

Men come home from their weekly bowling or golf match and are usually greeted by a caring woman who will usually ask, "How was your game? Did you have a good time?"

Sound familiar? The outcome of the game has an emotional element often misunderstood by men yet highly capitalized on by the FU.

The man who has a poor score may respond with any number of quips to the woman's query:

- "Don't ask, can you get me a drink?"
- "It sucked, can you get me a drink?"
- "You know my team mates, they couldn't keep up. Can you get me a drink?"
- He might just act with a little disdain at the question and brush past her in a huff as he grabs a cold one from the fridge.

The point is that guys who don't measure up to some expectation in their own minds consider their efforts a failure… which never goes unnoticed by the FU. The man has basically made it clear that he is emotionally vulnerable. He can't say, "Look at me! I'm the best!" What he has said instead is clearly an indication of failure on his part, but it is usually interpreted by the FU as any number of things. So look again at the statements above for what the man said and then read below what the woman probably heard:

- "I fell down and scraped my knee. It really hurts. Can you kiss it and make it better?"
- "I can't do anything right. Can I have some cookies to help me forget?"
- "The other guys were picking on me. Maybe a hug will make me feel better."

There are an infinite number of variants on the above. Simply put, men have expressed disappointment in a failure of their performance which is an expression of emotional need. The FU responds, usually with something nurturing. The act of nurturing is an act of "approval". Not approval of the failure – it's an approval (recognition) of the emotional need.  This is extremely powerful, and women know it!

Men can't get the same nurturing approval for their emotional need from other men.  Other guys will often give the normal pat on the back with a little comment like "you'll do better next time."  Or maybe a resounding "we'll get them next week."

The man who wins his golf or bowling match has probably already high-fived his team mates and been congratulated by the losing team.  The winning group will probably brag a little and recount the great moments during the game that really made them feel like superior competitors while sipping a cold beverage before heading home.  They will bask in the glory for a few minutes – "look at me, look at me."

The woman will know by the way the door opens and closes, and the way the man walks through the house that the man has been victorious. There are subtle signs and almost every man gives off the same aura when he has had a worthy accomplishment. The level of accomplishment can make this display very vivid and exciting at times. This is true for most accomplishments. It doesn't really matter if it was bowling, hunting, fishing or work related – if the man is pleased with himself it will show.

Men don't usually look quite as ostentatious as the male Frigate Bird who will puff out the huge red pouch on his throat as he dances and shakes to impress his female, but make no mistake, there will be a display.

The man usually can't wait to be asked how his day went. He may begin blurting out the accomplishment and the entire subtle nuance that went into his victory. The woman will watch and listen. She may nod her approval and offer to get the man a cold drink or fix his favorite meal to help him feel special while he recounts his day.

She is carefully attentive and observant during the "look at me" phase. She knows the man is seeking her approval whether he realizes it or not. He wants and clearly needs this emotional feeding by getting the woman's recognition.

Men expect women to see and approve everything they do. A man washes and waxes the family car and he expects his wife and kids to notice. He mows the lawn, trims the bushes and edges the walk ways and again, he expects the woman to notice and nod her approval. In fact, most guys will find an opportunity to point out these simple accomplishments.

So what? Well, a huge percentage of the women's magazines in the FU spend an enormous amount of time on how women "feel" unappreciated or under appreciated. Remember the three types of self-help quizzes? This is part of the psyche section.

Women, it turns out, require approval as much as men. Women in the FU generally won't say "look at me". Women tend to be exceedingly quiet when it comes to their own accomplishments. Oh sure, the big promotion or announcement that "I'm pregnant" or "I'm engaged" will usually have their moment. What you don't hear as much is who won on her bowling league or bridge club. You probably won't hear her saying "look at me" when she's finished cleaning the house from top to bottom or taking care of the millions of details in getting ready for Christmas or getting kids enrolled for the new school year.

Women could learn a little from men… Perhaps they should learn how to puff out their chests and loudly proclaim their accomplishments.

## Mark Dobbs

Men basically suck at being supportive when the women in their lives have had a bad day at work or rough day with the kids, or maybe they've lost an important tennis match. Guys usually respond to women with the same kind of rhetoric they use on other guys – which doesn't really answer the mail. "Practice makes perfect…" or "No pain, no gain…" or "Keep your chin up…"

The bottom line is that women have the same basic need for approval that most men have. They want men to notice the freshly cleaned house, the wonderfully prepared dinner (tastes are relative, be careful) and they want men to ask, "How was your day?"

The evolving male asks, "How was your day?" and remains attentive for a period of time to hear a recap of the entire day's events. Nodding frequently while eating dinner is perfectly acceptable, just remember the nodding rules from earlier in the book.

Navigating the Female Universe

The evolving male may also have learned to notice when the house has been freshly cleaned and be willing to offer an approving, "The house looks nice." A truly small reward for the woman, yet all too often overlooked by most men. This behavior may also earn "redeemable points" in some relationships. (See the next chapter on Making Points.)

Simply stated: Women in the FU need recognition and approval just as much as men…

Perhaps more!

The evolved male realizes that women have a completely different motivation for doing some things and that they see men's actions differently than most men intend them to be seen. This is the, "Did you do that for me?" conundrum. Be very careful as you learn how to navigate through this.

A man landscapes and manicures his yard to impress his family and his neighbors and to keep the city zoning commission from writing him a nuisance ticket. Primarily he does it to gain approval from his wife and others through the "look at me" method. A woman understands this need and responds appropriately.

But when a woman wants the man to help her clean house or deal with some other chore she somehow forgets that the man needs the "look at me" phase and approval that comes with it. Instead the woman usually offers the words, "Can't you do this for me?" Most men feel that this phrase is dramatic and see it as a threat. Let's face it, the question is loaded. There is only one answer the woman wants to hear – anything else is WRONG.

In the FU women believe that ***men should want*** to do things for women to make women feel appreciated. What women really need to do to get help around the house is to make the work about the man's need for approval instead of the woman's need to feel appreciated.

## Navigating the Female Universe

Of course the problem with men who do evolve a bit and develop some skills with housekeeping, laundry, or cooking is that women will brag to other women about what their newly trained or evolving man is doing. Perhaps the man finds out that he likes to cook and begins preparing wonderful meals occasionally for his family or friends. The next thing you know, the woman brags to other women and suddenly other women are now telling their less evolved men that they should be more like the other woman's man and then anarchy breaks out.

Guys who try to be more evolved will get teased by other, less evolved men. So while they may get the approval of a loving woman or family, they may somehow feel diminished around other men. Evolving men need to realize this is normal. Accept the behavior and have fun with it. Perhaps, when confronted with the new skill, the man should revert back to the "look at me" phase with the other guys.

Here's an approach to try with the guys, "Look, I actually do a pretty good job of cooking, and most of it is on the barbeque grill anyway. It keeps my wife from hassling me about leaving my dirty underwear all over the house and the sex is better than ever. Who knew that you could turn on a woman by cooking a little once in a while?" Once you make this a trade off that shows you still have the apparent upper hand somehow they will most likely relent. They may even ask for some recipes, especially if they believe there may be better sex as a reward to a new found skill.

---

***Seventh lesson**: In the FU, women would like their accomplishments to be seen by men with the same exuberance that men expect to receive from women and other men for theirs. Women who want men to help them with household chores should find a way to make it about the man's need for approval and* *not make it about some emotional need to have the man doing something "for her".*

# Chapter 8

# The Point System

The evolving man has stumbled around and by trial and error made some headway while attempting to navigate the FU. One of the more effective tools that many men have found seems to be the so-called "Point System." Some men believe that points are earned when they willingly do things that the man might otherwise consider undesirable.

Men using the Point System believe they can manipulate their position with women by accumulating points and then cashing them in like some sort of trading stamps. Once they've accumulated a certain level of points they may believe they have earned the right to have a weekend fishing trip with their buddies or perhaps a week away at duck hunting or deer hunting camp. Men with wives or serious partners seem to believe that

*Navigating the Female Universe*

they need permission to do things that don't include the wife or partner. Rather than going into the discussion with their wife or girl friend empty handed – the evolving man believes that he can somehow redeem his earned "points" and barter for a better position in the ensuing deliberation.

There may not be any real number value to the points, but the man knows when the level is worthy of his next selfish pursuit. The points are earned in many different ways. For demonstration purposes here are a few example actions with assumed point values assigned:

| | |
|---|---|
| Taking partner to a French restaurant: | 10 |
| Dinner and a movie: | 15 |
| Dinner and a movie she chooses: | 30 |
| Helping with cleaning house: | 10 |
| Helping in house without being asked: | 20 |
| Going shopping with your wife: | 10 |
| Going shopping for your wife: | 15 |
| Going to the Opera: | 50 |

| | |
|---|---|
| Going to the Ballet: | 75 |
| Having dinner with the in-laws: | 25 |

Men should not expect to earn points for doing things generally expected of them. Examples include but are not limited to - Birthday cards and/or gifts; Anniversary cards and/or gifts; Christmas cards and/or gifts; Picking up after yourself (that means dirty clothes in hamper, putting down the toilet seat, empty beer cans in the trash, etc. etc.); Any chore designated as yours (may include lawn work, car work, dinner dishes, etc. etc.); Time spent with children, pets or your own parents.

So let's say that the evolving man who has put himself on a Point System wants to go deer hunting for a week during Thanksgiving or perhaps buy season tickets to the ballpark. He may believe that this is going to require a huge trade in of points. He will start early in the year and begin planning how he will earn the trip. In his mind he may believe that the hunting trip will require 100 points to equalize his bartering position. Therefore, he may choose to go to the ballet and have dinner with the in-laws without a complaint.

He doesn't argue or complain because he accepts that his apparent willingness to do these things will improve his bartering position.

Simple! Efficient! ***Potentially dangerous.***

There are a few things every man needs to know about the Point System before beginning or continuing to use it:

- Women who realize that the Point System is in play may begin deducting points for perceived bad behavior. The more the woman tries to change a man's behavior, the more points will likely be reduced. Remember the chapter "Simple Creatures, Change Them All" – quote: "In the FU, there is a tremendous investment by women throughout the world to monitor men and modify them in whole or in part. Every change successfully manipulated is one more small victory in the woman's evolution of man. This isn't war, but sometimes you will feel like it is." Therefore, any new behavior modification successfully manipulated by the woman will not be eligible for points in the future.

- When a man willingly goes to the opera and then appears to enjoy the event, the woman will not agree that points have been earned. The same applies to any event or action where the man actually likes whatever it is that he is doing. So, if you like your in-laws, no points. If you like the ballet, no points. If you like shopping for lingerie with your wife or girl friend, no points. If you like shopping for lingerie without your wife or girlfriend then you might want to look for a different book.

If you haven't developed any other system to help you negotiate with your woman, remember she's a fully vested member of the FU, then the Point System may be a good tool and could result in better negotiations when seeking approval. As long as the evolving man knows the basic rules of engagement he will do fine. Remember that actions which become repetitive and likeable soon lose value in the Point System and that the system only works in the FU while it remains a semi-covert tool. If you put a white board or chalk board up in the garage or man-cave and write down the activities and a running point tally – you will probably lose your edge and all previously earned points will be negated.

-------------------------------------------------

***Eighth lesson:*** *In the FU, whatever goes up can come crashing down.*

# Chapter 9

# Asking for Directions or Any Help for that Matter

Everyone knows that most guys WON'T stop and ask for directions and that these same guys will try almost everything before asking for any kind of help for that matter. It's a basic male instinct. Guys just know that asking for help shows some kind of lack of independence or weakness and seems to be a last resort. Asking for help is only done when all other options have been carefully considered and probably exhausted.

The FU believes that this lack of willingness to ask for help as an early solution to any problem is a weakness or flaw in the male psyche. Women will stop and ask for directions after they perceive themselves to be lost and quite simply don't understand why men can't do the same. Asking for help in the FU is an early option to solve most problems.

There are dozens of psychological studies on this phenomenon. There was even a study performed in England which seemed to show that men drive an average of nearly three hundred extra miles in a lifetime while lost just to prevent asking for directions.

Another theory is that women have a lesser developed sense of direction and freely accept their condition sooner than men. It has also been argued that women tend to get lost more frequently than men and that the simple act of being lost is more emotionally frightening for women, therefore, women have adapted by asking for help to prevent feeling frightened.

Men may believe that women get lost easier and need help more often; however, this factor should never be discussed. Women will generally explain that they usually prepare better for traveling than men and that their willingness to ask for help is a survival mechanism that prevents wanton waste of either time or resources. Women will also argue that men are not willing to admit when they are lost because that is something akin to being wrong and being wrong is clearly a failure at some very elemental level.

Men and women are clearly different on this issue and it is a long standing and highly debated behavior. The "debates" about this behavior have probably ended relationships between men and women on more than one occasion and almost every sitcom on TV has offered at least one short story involving this lack of willingness by men to ask for directions.

Men need to simply accept the fact that a woman will begin pressing the man to ask for directions as soon as she is aware, or instinctively believes that the man is lost. She's not trying to be evil. It's her nature. Just like it's the man's nature to avoid asking.

The resulting conflict comes from the fact that the woman, who seems to have almost unlimited abilities to control her usual environment, finds herself feeling threatened by a loss of control. The man is lost, the woman is lost and the woman can't tolerate the feeling of being out of control. She's going to ask, she has to ask, it becomes inevitable.

Eons of evolution or the basic male and female building blocks from creation have left this rather touchy subject with us to be considered for the foreseeable future without any realistic compromise or solution – until now!

Men driving by themselves may continue driving lost until they regain control of their natural sense of direction. Men with women (it doesn't matter whether the woman is a wife, girlfriend, work mate, sister, or mother) will have to be creative to keep the woman from going to critical mass. The following actions are recommended:

- Review your travel plan well before beginning your trip to make sure you know the route.
- Tell the woman you are going to be traveling with that you're not sure of the directions and that she should have them written out for easy reference before commencing the trip. This does not admit weakness and will be interpreted by women as wise and seen by other men as "delegating work" which is a perfectly acceptable behavior.
- Program a GPS or other device to assist you.
- Ask the woman to drive. This is very empowering for women and will result in the woman thinking that you are a more sensitive and highly evolved male. If she

admits that she doesn't know the way to the destination then use the moment to seek directions from a reliable source before getting on the road. The total of these actions will strengthen her belief that you are somehow more evolved then most other men.

If you fail to do anything and become lost you may try the following:

- Argue with the woman and explain that you know where you are generally, but the exact location is a bit less clear and then ask if she can do any better. She will tell you where to go.
- Ask the woman to use a cell phone to call for directions. She will tell you where to go.
- Stop to get a soft drink and use the restroom. This will allow the woman time to ask for directions while you're

"busy". When you return to the car she will tell you where to go.

Bottom line – if you don't do anything… she will tell you where to go and the despondent debate will undoubtedly ensue.

---

***Ninth lesson:*** *In the FU, knowing how to get where you're going is preferable to being told "where to go."*

# Chapter 10

## The Shopping Conundrum

If your back hurts just thinking about shopping with a woman then you're part of a huge majority of men struggling to survive in the FU.

What are the options?

Most men think that accepting an invitation to shop with a woman is somehow an act of advanced evolution. That simple act may have been seen as an evolved behavior when Jackie "O" was in vogue, but shopping opportunities and facilities have changed tremendously over the last thirty of forty years.

Gone are the days when shopping meant going to Sears, Macy's, or Penny's. Even a simple shopping mall with a giant retailer as an anchor store is a waning concept. Today's shopping opportunities vary from the creative and entertaining like the Mall of America to the simple retro downtown shopping experience like a Promenade or generically "The Shops at…" (pick your favorite location near a lake or river).

Shopping today is overwhelming. Young kids at every corner hanging out to be cool with their friends. People are lined up to eat, watch movies or play video games. It seems that most shopping areas are bustling centers for every kind of activity to entertain people. Oh yeah, and some still focus on retail sales.

If you plan to be successful in the FU then it's important to recognize the shopping conundrum and how best to navigate through the possible entanglements.

Guys need to understand that a woman in the FU will invite their man to go shopping as an act of courtesy. Shopping is an important act for many women. When a woman asks if you want to go – she does it for several reasons. Most of the reasons won't make sense to most men. So instead, let's focus on different shopping types and possible opportunities for men to participate and still avoid the dreaded back ache.

When it's time to do the weekly shopping for groceries and household items the woman might see this as a duty or chore and may expect that it should be shared with her man like housework. If you're married or in a fulltime housekeeping relationship with a woman who has a full time job outside of the home then you should consider participating in the activity. Yes, the evolving male will concede on this and participate to some degree.

When you do decide to venture out, make sure there's a shopping list. Try to direct the shopping to a modern mega-mart where they have automotive supplies, hunting, fishing, hardware and yard care items as well as food. When you get to the store volunteer to speed up the process and take part of the list and head off on your own. Divide and conquer! You will have plenty of time for a little self indulgence.

After you're out of the woman's sight you're free to cruise the fishing and hunting supplies or check out the latest gadgets for cleaning and waxing the family car or your old sports car. You might even be able to catch part of the ball game on TV in the electronics section of the store or just browse the magazine racks for the latest edition of your favorite mag.

WATCH YOUR TIME! Keep track of how long you're gone. Your woman will likely be reviewing labels, talking to friends they run into, comparing prices, reviewing coupons and all sorts of activities that will slow her down and otherwise cause your back to ache if you stay with her. Just be careful, give yourself time to get back to the shopping you were supposed to be doing and then catch up with your shopping mate to compare notes and find out what else may be needed before ending the outing.

If you're invited for a day trip of non-household shopping – better known as a "shop 'til you drop" day, then be very careful and review all the options before answering. Remember the chapter about women wanting to do certain activities with other women – this is usually one of those activities. Before answering the question about going you should ask her if she would prefer to just go on her own or with some of her friends. You might find out that she was just being polite and that she really would like to go with "the girls". Remember, women may ask a man as a courtesy and not actually expect or want him to go. Don't be too willing to accept the invitation until you've actually talked to her about the details.

By the way, here's a short note about women showing this "courtesy" type behavior of asking the man to go shopping with her. Women who use this tactic expect the man to reciprocate. When you're getting ready for a golf, fishing or hunting outing – she wants you to ask her if she wants to go. She probably won't go unless she happens to like to hunt, fish or golf but she expects the same courtesy she showed you when she asked if you wanted to go shopping. You can obviously imagine the numerous iterations. Use this tactic sparingly and only when you can accommodate the woman. If you've made plans for a "guys only" deal then let her know that you would like for her to go, but sadly "the guys have already made plans". Perhaps you and she can go together the next time.

If the woman doesn't have any plans to shop with other women and sincerely wants your company for the day then you need to consider several things. For example:

- How many points is this worth?

- Will there be stores where you're going that you can lose yourself in? Perhaps a Cabela's, Gander Mountain, L.L. Bean or Bass Pro Shops.
- Will you be rewarded later? Sex? Good food? Sex?
- Is there a sports bar or casino in the shopping area?

A day of shopping in the FU, relaxing at a restaurant with your woman afterwards and listening to her numerous shopping conquests will be rewarding. Especially if there's a big sale on at Cabela's!

---

***Tenth lesson***: *In the FU, sharing household chores, including grocery shopping is the sign of an evolving male. Asking your partner "first" to share in a pastime activity is a true courtesy. Expecting*

***him or her to share in the activity is just self centered.***

# Chapter 11

# A Simple Yes or No is All I Want

While navigating through the FU you will undoubtedly stumble upon a realization that women almost never answer straight forward questions with a simple YES or NO. At some point you will find yourself angered by this behavior.

Just because many women can't seem to give a simple answer to a generally simple question doesn't mean it's a FU conspiracy. It is a basic psychological safeguard that these women genuinely don't usually realize they are employing.

Some women have realized that not giving a simple yes or no answer is seemingly evasive and they have learned that answering a question with a question will buy them time before answering the first question. This delay tactic may even gain them more info about the person's motives for asking the question to begin with. It is an unnerving behavior that gives the women massive amounts of power.

Be warned – there is not a defense against this behavior. Men who try to play the "answer the question with a question" game will only anger the woman and incur her wrath… probably the silent treatment.

Just accept the fact that the average man cannot win the "answer the question with a question" game. What's left? Here are a few ways that the evolving modern man may safely navigate the simple answer to a simple question phenomenon:

- Only ask a question when you have plenty of time for an answer.
- While listening to the answer practice the nodding techniques learned earlier in this guide.

- Pay close attention for key words in her monologue that could indicate other, more significant issues. Some of the words include: Mother, Children, Work, Money, Late Period, Tired, Pregnant, New Boyfriend, Leaving You, You're so Stupid, You Never Listen... Some of these words may be clues that better advice and professional counseling is needed.

The evolving man may try shortening the initial question. For example:

- Instead of, "Would you like to have dinner at that new Italian restaurant tonight?" Try, "Dinner?"

Short questions could result in a quick answer followed with a short question. For example:

- Your shortened question: "Dinner?"
- Her answer: "Sure, where?"

- Your response: "New Italian place. We can leave around six-thirty'ish." You should be walking away or appear busy starting a lawn mower or vacuum cleaner at this point to avoid her next level of questions or responses. Some women are turned on by the direct "take charge" approach AND most women are turned on by men using a vacuum cleaner...

Notice the simplicity of the shortened question.

An analysis of the longer version of the example question above shows several pitfalls that you need to recognize. By recognizing them you may be able to avoid the pitfalls in all future questions, unless of course you happen to have time and are a really good listener.

Here are some of the pitfalls in the longer version of the sample question. It started with "Would you like..." Any word in a question that connotes a desire to discover ***feelings*** is always dangerous. Asking the average woman if she "would like" something will get you a range of responses about her general feelings concerning the subject and probably experiences with previous similar events. By combining the question of "like" with the "new Italian restaurant" you have combined an emotional prompt with an information sharing prompt. Any "new" thing in the FU will have already been dissected by others and reported to the masses. This will garner a response concerning the unsubstantiated quality of the restaurant and an emotional rally concerning prior experiences with "new" restaurants.

The bottom line is that you will hear several minutes of what the woman feels like now or will feel like later about eating dinner at a restaurant that has probably already stirred rumor or conjecture. You will have opened a door about what other things may be on her mind concerning the period of time around dinner that she may have already preplanned. Such pre-planning may have involved children, friends, parents, work, favorite TV show, and so on.

If you chose this path – be prepared to listen and try to comprehend enough to know whether there is an actual answer in the response. Sometimes there is. Sometimes there isn't. Don't act like you're listening and then rephrase the question and ask again just because you weren't listening. Also, as a reminder for the less evolved men – if you smell some form of food already cooking, don't ask about going out to dinner, especially if the "aroma" is unrecognizable. (There's no excuse for stupidity no matter what Universe you're trying to navigate.)

-------------------------------------------------

***<u>Eleventh lesson</u>: In the FU, short and simple only applies to men.***

# Chapter 12

## Beer Isn't a Food Group

There are multiple factions of people arguing about various diets these days. Vegans, vegetarians, low-carb eaters, high protein people, gluten free dieters, etc., etc. All have valid arguments about the benefits of what they support. This chapter isn't meant to criticize or support any specific type of diet. The intent is to simply recognize that what may be good for some isn't always good for everyone. It also recognizes that everyone has different tastes and that everyone tastes things differently. In short, people are amazingly diverse when it comes to diet.

Men will eat what pleases them. More evolved men will find a thing to eat that both pleases them AND is "approved" as healthy for them. And, although a bit controversial, some men believe that beer provides at least some "food" value while regular food doesn't provide any "beer" value.

As you begin to evolve you will no doubt find that the FU has concluded through multitudes of studies that red wine is clearly better for you than beer and may try to make you appear more civilized at social functions by insisting that you share in a glass of red wine. Don't argue, the research is overwhelming, you will lose. Just shut-up and drink the wine. The beer will still be there later. You'll be able to wash away all the grape juice when you get home.

If you're in a relationship with an active member of the FU there will be a discussion concerning eating and drinking behaviors at some point. This may or may not have anything to do with anyone's weight or current health status. The discussion will come up usually because the woman has recently read a new magazine piece on some special diet or watched a particularly enlightening episode of Dr. What's His Name's show. Of course, if either the man or the woman (or both) have a bit of a health or weight issue then this conversation will likely have a much more emotional element.

Men need to understand that every woman has the same basic instinct to nurture those people around her that she cares about as she would her own child. If the woman has prepared a new "healthy" dinner as a surprise for her loving man, then the loving man needs to know how to respond without being derisive. It is important to remember that the woman may be trying a new diet for her own benefit, however, in her mind it will be for the benefit of her loved ones… and that includes you.

If you make fun of her new project or demean her effort in any way, you will be insulting her ability to nurture. It won't have anything to do with the food being prepared, or new healthful program, or anticipated benefits that you're dismissing – she will only hear that you are attacking her ability to nurture and do what's best for her family.

While navigating the FU, men need to understand that food doesn't just satisfy physical hunger only. Food, it seems, has a huge emotional angle. Volumes of psychiatric work have been done about human being's emotional connections to food. This emotional element is true for men and women. How many times have you heard the term "comfort food"? Sometimes, food satisfies us more than simply filling our bellies.

The truly evolved man will share in menu planning and try to comprehend the health benefits of the dietary changes and then be as supportive as possible. Most women interested in losing weight sometimes forget that a calorie restricted menu that is designed for women to lose pounds is simply not enough food for the average sized man. Also, men tend to be less critical of themselves and their size and may not have faced their pending health issues by the time the woman has developed a new course of action.

More women than men (as a percentage of the total) suffer from body dysmorphic disorder. Actually, some research indicates that more people have this disorder than are willing to admit. In fact, almost everyone sees themselves in the mirror just a bit differently than other people see them. It seems that perhaps the visual cortex in our brains is affected (or protected) by our psyche's ability to alter "self" image.

What does all this mean? Simply, that man will likely have to answer the age-old and time tested question from a woman they love that usually goes like this: "Do these jeans make my butt look big?"

How do you answer that?

How do you answer that and keep a relationship intact?

Navigating the Female Universe

Truthful answers aren't always smart. Here are some despicably wrong answers:

- No, the "jeans" don't make your butt look big…
- Yes…
- They seem a little tight…
- What do you mean by "big"?
- Big is beautiful…
- What size are those jeans? (Like you would know the difference anyway, and you probably don't know what she "believes" should be "her size".)

The correct answer – "I love the way you look in anything and nothing at all is even better." (Warning – this may not work in all circumstances.)

Anyway, back to something a bit simpler – food. The evolving man probably recognizes that various foods provide differing levels of nutrition and that certain foods are less healthful than others.

## Mark Dobbs

Regardless of an individual's belief in eating or avoiding red meat, or any meat for that matter, it is safe to say that not all people recognize the benefits of all the food groups supported by the USDA's food pyramid. Even the food pyramid has evolved over the last twenty years.

Moderation, it seems, is still the safest rule for almost everything you eat or drink. Excesses of almost anything tend to be precursors for future problems. Take carrots for example. Carrots, as everyone knows are believed to be good for you. They are rich in beta-carotene and fiber, the beta-carotene metabolizes in humans into Vitamin A and carrots contain numerous minerals good for most of us. They are mildly sweet when ripe; contain some protein and taste pretty darn good. However, eating carrots in excess can cause carotenosis which is a massive build up of the beta-carotene in the body which then turns the skin orange! So, even eating carrots in excess is not necessarily a good thing. Of course, no one has ever died from being orange.

---------------------------------------------------

***Twelfth lesson:** In the FU, food, just like love, is a nurturing tool. Unlike love, too much food can be as bad as too little.*

# Chapter 13

# The FU Thinks Men Have a Hearing Problem and Perhaps a Little Vision Impairment Too

What is this hearing problem?

Women seem to believe that when they have something to say (which is more frequently than they will admit) that what they say must be important and men should be listening. For most men, not hearing everything a woman says is not so much about the function of hearing as it is about attention or perception.

Men listen. For the most part, men have excellent hearing, or at least they have excellent auditory receptive potential. Of course there are exceptions according to age, genetics and damage from noise exposure or other environmental or physical difficulties.

The FU simply will not accept that a man, any man, could possibly be distracted when a woman begins to speak. In reality, men are exceedingly and frequently distracted. Remember the chapter which suggests that all men are actually very simple creatures. Sometimes the distractions are complex issues about work, religion, or politics; but typically the distractions are much less complex. The distractions may even border on insanely simple.

Guys can be distracted by a growling stomach, thoughts of past sex, or thoughts of future sex. Perhaps he's thinking hard trying to hold in a big fart or belch, thinking of sex, thinking about the weekend of golf, fishing, hunting, football, NASCAR, the Final Four, and more sex of course. Sometimes men are distracted by a smell or sight (not always a pretty woman, but frequently). Many times guys simply lose their grip on the moment and "zone out". Zoning out is like meditating in public. The mind goes blank and a calming feeling takes over. Anything that is said in the direction of a man who is engaged in public meditation will be likely lost in the greater ethos never to be heard again.

Women expect men to listen… however, men can (and do) *appear* to listen without actually tuning in and *hearing* what is being said. Oh sure, evolving men have learned to stay tuned in enough to know when to nod at the right time. You remember, nod up and down to show understanding or agreement and nod side to side to show empathy or concern.

An evolving man who appears to be listening will still be distracted frequently but tries very hard to hear well enough to know when something is said that he is probably expected to answer or remember. Again, being a good listener really means being perceptive and hearing what needs to be heard.

Navigating the Female Universe

There is a very fine, sometimes indiscernible line between actively hearing and not listening. After all, sometimes in the FU the woman may simply need to monologue for a while and doesn't expect any intercourse (sorry, that means conversation for now). She may have a story to tell, rumor to pass or simply needs to dump a line of emotional baggage. However, occasionally you will find yourself receiving a monologue that turns into a dialogue where actual information is exchanged and some amount of thinking is required on your part. Successful navigation of the FU means you have to learn to discern between the two basic lines of communication.

There are pitfalls of course. Regardless of the form of communication there is a reasonable expectation which suggests that a woman in the FU will NOT simply monologue about something without interjecting some other coherent line of data that the man is supposed to somehow cull from the rest of the discourse. So as you evolve you will need to learn specific cues which indicate something is being said that is of relative importance and may require remembering. Once you learn the cues you will be closer to improving your overall hearing.

It is likely that anything you do to try and improve your appearance as a better listener will make you seem more evolved in the FU. Only time will tell how well you adapt. Typically, most men will settle back into a comfortable form of "adaptive censorship." That phrase sounds a little more evolved than "selective listener" don't you think? Adaptive censorship infers that men actively listen and hear everything and then censor out what they don't want to remember. Selective listener means that men only hear what they want to hear. Selective listeners are probably less evolved. Your choice. Either way, you're still in trouble if you miss something…and you will.

As for the vision problem?

Navigating the Female Universe

Well, for what it's worth – many women believe that men have a significant vision problem as well the little hearing issue. How many times have you gotten up from your favorite chair in front of the TV to go into the kitchen, opened the refrigerator, grabbed a drink or snack and returned to your chair and never once noticed what a typical woman might have seen or even done while making the same trip?

The average man can get out of the chair with the single thought of getting the drink and walk past or step over the kids toys or other things clearly not "put up" and then not see the spilled milk in the floor where the three year old just dumped his "tippy mug" or the stack of dirty dishes on the counter top by the full sink, the overflowing trash can, maybe some sticky hand prints on the refrigerator, and Fido's empty water dish and food bowl.

If the typical fully developed woman in the FU had offered to get you the drink it would have taken her twenty minutes. This statement isn't meant to be derogatory in any way. The simple truth is that she will probably see all the obstacles that your tunnel vision allowed you to miss and then she will deal with each one before finally getting your drink. In fact, she might become so engulfed in her environmental distractions that she will forget her initial mission (getting you a drink) and begin some other project that the minor obstacles reminded her about.

Most guys are target oriented. Once the mind is set to "get the drink," it's almost impossible for the average, less evolved, man to be diverted by minor obstacles. Most women simply have a much broader vision. They see the details in their environment and, when circumstances permit they try to maintain some control throughout the daily cycle.

Women who have the energy or emotional fortitude may attempt to shame their man into changing his vision problem. What happens? Once you've returned to your chair in front of the TV with that cold drink or crunchy snack the woman will shake her head or roll her eyes and may ask, "How could you just walk by that spilled milk?" Of course the lesser evolved man will answer, "I didn't see it." The woman will simply be incapable of understanding how anyone could not see IT and likely respond with, "Are you blind?" which could lead to a short discussion about your other shortcomings.

-------------------------------------------------

***<u>Thirteenth lesson</u>: In the FU, when you get caught not listening just admit that you were deep in thought. When she asks what you were thinking about – simply offer, "I was thinking about you." As for the Vision issue – try not to step in the spilled milk, it will reduce the appearance of your deficiency.***

# Chapter 14

## Compromise to Settlement

You have probably already realized that most of men's less evolved behaviors require some modification… at least as determined by members of the FU. Your ability to "compromise" with your female partner to work on any or all of the behaviors that *she believes* require changing will be the best indicator of your improved ability to navigate easier in the FU.

Learning to be an effective negotiator will improve your "compromising" position. Negotiation is the art of effective communication. It involves two parties capable of listening and hearing. It also requires that each person knows what is worth losing. Negotiation is not fighting. It is a verbal confrontation or debate that draws a metaphorical line in the sand which one party ultimately must cross before compromise can be reached.

Deliberation is a difficult and tedious process where each party must reflect on those things which have been discussed, including the balance of power and what may be gained or lost by crossing or not crossing the line in the sand. Deliberations should never take more than a day. Typically, one party or the other will start the deliberation process by stating, "Let's sleep on it." If deliberations go longer than a day then you can assume one of two things: 1) She forgot and you're safe for a while; or 2) You forgot and she'll be very angry. Either way, deliberations that go too long usually require a completely new negotiation phase.

Mediation is a tool which may be used to help one or both of the negotiators to get to a compromising position. Mediation normally involves a third party. Third parties should be someone considered to be neutral by each of the negotiators. This third party is called a mediator and may be a professional counselor, parole officer, psychologist, judge, or minister. Mediation should only be used as a last resort unless you're already under the control or management of one of these professionals. Mothers-in-law, other relatives, and any friends for that matter, are never, never mediators.

The final part of compromise is the "settlement". Settlement is what has been agreed to. Who gives up what behavior or accepts what behavior? Settlement is the treaty, pact, contract, or promise that seals the understanding between the parties and leads to harmony.

---

***Fourteenth lesson:*** *** In the FU, "compromise" usually means that the woman wins!***

# Chapter 15

## PMS Doesn't Stand for "Pissed at Men Syndrome"

Here's a short summary of what you should have gleaned from the Guide:

Basically, whether you agree or not, now you know that **women run the universe**. You also see that women could be considered superior by divine design. Women have a basic ability to see the deeper meaning behind even the simplest concept. Sex in the FU is all about relationships and emotional bonding and commitment before the physical act of sex is ever started. Women, as you undoubtedly know by now, clearly want to change you. Even the most evolved man will need some occasional changing. You've discovered that most men and women currently in heterosexual relationships still exhibit a bit of Gay or Lesbian tendency.

## Mark Dobbs

Guys typically need "acceptance and approval" for their accomplishments no matter how insignificant and women are much better at giving the kind of nurturing support that men (and children) need. Guys, however, generally fail to show reciprocal approval for women's efforts and accomplishments.

Some men believe that they can improve their position in a relationship by the use of a kind of bartering and that a rudimentary point system is in place to help them gain a better bargaining position. Women who become aware of the point system will learn quickly that they can change the balance of power by subtracting points for poor behavior.

Men have a better general sense of direction than women, however, are much less likely to admit when their internal compass has failed. Unlike men, women will ask for help without believing that the act of asking for help is akin to admitting failure. You also know that getting a simple answer to a question in the FU is nearly impossible. Yes and no answers must be qualified, usually at length. Only rarely will the extra explanation answer the original question.

Many men believe that beer has "food value" but food doesn't have any "beer value." Diet fads are generally directed by the FU and men almost always get what they need whether they want it or not.

The FU has very specific expectations about how well men should be able to hear. Listening and hearing aren't the same. And, most guys probably need some work with their vision issues according to most women.

Lastly, PMS really doesn't stand for Pissed at Men Syndrome. Women are sympathetic with other women during PMS, yet completely ready to launch an all out attack on a man who is simply unaware or not observing nature's greatest curse on women. So, if you're really just that lost about the signs and symptoms of Pre-Menstrual Syndrome and continue to do really stupid things during these short "periods" that happen almost every twenty-eight days or so, then you deserve what you get – this isn't rocket science. By the way, for the new fathers out there... if you are blessed with one or more daughters – there is a phenomenon where all the women who live close together can actually synchronize their PMS. Believe me; it will make weaker men quiver.

---

***Fifteenth lesson:*** *In the FU, give a man a fish and he will eat for a day; teach a man to fish and he will have a new way to totally anger his female partner.*

# Epilogue

## For Women Only

Owing to the simple fact that women will be reading this guide – it is important to point out some poignant truths. Please, if your man is attempting or considering the evolutionary process and learning how to navigate in the FU – try to understand how difficult and far the journey really seems to him. For some guys, the journey can be epic. Here are a few simple truths to remember:

- Men are NOT mind readers.
- Crying IS blackmail.
- Ask for what you want. Let us be clear on this one: Subtle hints do not work! Strong hints do not work! Obvious hints do not work! Just ask for what you want.
- Yes and No are perfectly acceptable answers to almost every question.

- If you share a problem with a man, he will try to solve it. Sympathy is what your girlfriends are for.
- Anything we said 6 months ago is inadmissible in an argument.
- If something we said can be interpreted two ways and one of the ways makes you angry, then we meant <u>the other one</u>.
- You can either ask us to do something or tell us how you want it done. Not both. If you already know best how to do it, just do it yourself.
- Christopher Columbus did <u>NOT</u> need directions and neither do most men.
- If it itches, it <u>will</u> be scratched. Men do that, sometimes in public.
- If a man asks what is wrong and a woman says "nothing," then men will act like nothing's wrong. The man knows you are lying, but it is just not worth the hassle.

*Navigating the Female Universe*

- If you ask a question that you really don't want answered, then expect an answer you don't want to hear.
- Don't ask men what they're thinking about unless you are prepared to discuss such topics as Football, Hockey, fishing, hunting or work.
- Most men believe they are "in shape." <u>Round</u> IS a shape!
- Sleeping on the couch is like camping; most men don't really mind it that much.


(*These observations are not credited to any one person. They are a culmination of many thoughts collected over the years from many sources.)

Mark Dobbs

# **Afterword**

Well, that's the long and short of it. This "Guide" is a simple beginning, a stepping off point, the first cast, the kick-off, tee shot, puck-drop, tip-off, or whatever. It won't keep you from making mistakes along the way, no guide can do that. But perhaps the next time you're sitting in the garage or man cave or your favorite watering hole contemplating why your female partner is "pissed" at you, maybe this guide might give you a hint at where you went wrong.

The guide certainly doesn't attempt to cover every possible nuance of behavior in the FU and even if it did women would continue to change and surprise most men anyway. Change, so it would seem, is just part of the greater design in the FU.

Also, if you are making the effort to evolve you will see that many men will continue to behave in an un-evolved manner regardless of how much they read or get badgered by their partner. Don't be dissuaded by them, you make your own decisions. Some men can't or won't change; others are much slower to change. Women will continue to love them and show acceptance of their poor behavior hoping that someday the man will relent to even the most subtle changes because in the FU women are rewarded for even the slightest change in a man's behavior, no matter how much pain and anguish the man must endure.

Evolution is a slippery slope. Sometimes you will go backwards even when you think you've tried very hard to go forward. You will likely make mistakes. Mistakes are an expected part of the process and as long as you're willing to recognize which mistakes "she thinks" you've made and show some willingness to apologize for them you should be okay.

# Glossary

**Andropause** – This is male menopause. Yes, men have a hormonal change of life too. Some call it "low T". This doesn't happen at a general age among men. Some men never actually experience this phenomenon.

**Points** – Imaginary scoring system used by some men to gain some perceived tactical advantage in negotiating with women.

**Nodding, Horizontal** – Moving your head by rotating from side. This generally indicates a non-verbal empathy or sympathy for what is being said

**Nodding, Vertical** – Moving your head by raising and lowering your chin in the vertical direction. This is a nonverbal indication that you're listening and understanding what is being said.

## Navigating the Female Universe

**PMS** – Does not mean "Pissed at Men Syndrome" even though it causes the same emotional, physical and psychotic behavior and can be misdiagnosed by an un-evolved man. Never ask a woman if she's PMSie when *your* behavior has very clearly caused the symptoms.

**Romance** – The pleasurable feeling of excitement and mystery associated with a loving relationship. In the context of romantic love relationships, romance usually implies an expression of one's love, or one's deep emotional desires to connect with another person.

**Romantic** – The act or acts of romance. Generally, this means doing things to imply your loving desire for the other person. Romantic acts may be considered sexy by some women (see definition of sexy below).

**Sexy (Men's Definition)** – Basically, sexy is any female form that is in any way appealing to the man being asked. Naked is sexy, diaphanous clothing on a woman is sexy, lingerie is sexy, pajamas are sexy, tight jeans are sexy, short skirts are sexy. Sexy also includes high heels, bare feet, daisy dukes, halter tops, bikinis, cheerleader costumes, black stockings, women in uniform, women in work out gear, women hunting, women fishing, women golfing, women using some power tools.... In fact, most things about a woman's body and her attempt to cover some or all of it and her participation in any activity could be considered sexy by most horny virile men.

**Sexy (Women's Definition)** – Generally, sexy is defined as anything that enhances a female's sexual attraction to someone. The attraction may be to a person's looks or movements or to their voice or smell, perhaps their conversation ability and numerous other factors. The attraction may be enhanced by a person's financial or professional status, clothing, cologne, hair style, and anything else which can attract the sexual interest of another person. Some women consider certain behaviors sexy. Any man showing compassion to children, old people, animals, and giving away an easy smile could be considered sexy. Sometimes the activities of men are considered sexy by some women. This can range from bad boy biker, rodeo cowboy, a man pushing a vacuum cleaner, or even a professional male exotic dancer. Go figure.

**Hamper** – This is a housekeeping tool. Usually found in a bedroom closet, bathroom, linen closet or laundry room. It is generally used to collect soiled clothing awaiting laundering. Women want men to use them. If you don't use one now this may be your first step in evolving. Get one, use it – gain points.

**Adaptive Censorship** – When men discuss their relative ability to actually hear and comprehend things said by women, this term indicates the man is an active listener and hears everything but chooses what he will somehow censor from his memory. It doesn't indicate that the censorship was correct or good – just that he was in control of the process.

**Selective Hearing** – This term indicates an un-evolved man hasn't learned how to listen and he only seems to hear what his instinctive lesser evolved self is willing to hear.

**Intercourse** – For the purposes of this book this is a descriptive term used to indicate a relationship by two-way communication both verbally and non-verbally. If sex happens to be part of the intercourse then it could be intercourse with intercourse. Clear?

**Fine** – Word used to end an argument when she is right and you need to shut up.

**Five Minutes** – For her if she is getting dressed this means half an hour. For you watching the game it means five minutes.

**Nothing** – This is the answer to "What's wrong" indicating the calm before the storm, you did something wrong and she knows it. You need to be on your toes.

**Go Ahead** – You actually ask to go do something that you already know she doesn't like, but she says "go ahead" - this is a dare, not permission. Don't do it.

**Loud Sigh** – This is a word in the FU. It means you're an idiot and she wonders why she is wasting her time arguing with you.

**That's Okay** – Very dangerous statement that means she wants to think long and hard before deciding how and when you will pay for your mistake.

**Thanks** – Just say, "you're welcome."

**Thanks a Lot** – This is sarcasm, don't say, "you're welcome."

**Don't worry about it** – If you hear this then you're in trouble. She has told you do something several times, you didn't remember or didn't listen and now she's going to do it herself. You'll probably ask her what's wrong and she'll reply, "Nothing".

## Mark Dobbs

**One bagger** – The man will successfully have sex if the woman puts a bag over her head so that her looks don't spoil the moment.

**Two bagger** – The man will successfully have sex if the woman puts a bag over her head and the man wears a bag just in case the woman's bag breaks.

**Coyote ugly** – You wake up with your arm under her and you realize that she's so ugly that you decide to chew off your own arm rather than wake her up when you're trying to get out of the bedroom.

Navigating the Female Universe

# Men's Self Help Test

This "Self Help" test has not been evaluated at any academic level. It shouldn't be...

The test is meant to see if men can determine their own level of evolution as it may pertain to navigating the FU. The test will lead to a general characterization of most men.

The only test question you are faced with is this:

***Will you take a self-help test?***

**A.** If you ***WILL*** take the test:

   1. You probably believe you are fully evolved and want to see if you can *Ace* the test. If you believe you are fully evolved and have a competitive "look-at-me" need to prove you can Ace the test... then you're probably only posing as a fully evolved male. Go ahead and Ace the test! The proof of partial evolution will earn you points in the FU.

OR

    2. You are interested in evolving on your own. Showing an interest in evolving will earn points in the FU.

OR

    3. The woman in your life is forcing you to take the test to reinforce her belief that you're either not evolved or only partly evolved meaning there's room for improvement. Taking the test "for her" shows you are willing to listen and accommodate the woman and therefore earn you points in the FU.

OR

    4. You're looking at the test and basically faking taking it. You're hoping a woman sees you so that she thinks you're trying to evolve and perhaps that will spark her to be more interested in you. You're probably single or not in a serious long-term

relationship yet. The points you gain won't really matter, but you might get "lucky".

**B.** If you ***WON'T*** take the test:

1. You're afraid of change and afraid that the other guys may see you thinking about evolving and accuse you of being weak.

OR

2. You're completely comfortable in your less evolved state which means that your life hasn't been challenged hard by the FU yet or that your female partner has basically accepted your remaining faults and passes them off as "cute" to other members of the FU.

OR

3. You could be fully evolved and are perusing the questions with your female partner while drinking a glass of red wine, having a Vegan dinner, and laughing at lesser evolved men.

## *TEST COMPLETE*

For purposes of discussion with your female partner please write in your general personal characterization from the answers above:_____

_____

_____

_____

_____

(Please make sure your partner reads the Epilogue of this guide before engaging in any real conversation with you about your evolutionary process.)

# All the Lessons In the FU...

***First lesson:*** An un-evolved man is, and always will be an unarmed man in the FU.

***Second lesson:*** In the FU, women generally see deeper meanings in everything and what men see isn't always what they get!

***Third lesson:*** In the FU, nodding appropriately is a key communication tool for men. Keep the conversation focused on the woman.

***Fourth lesson:*** In the FU, successful sexual coupling means engaging in relationships and romance. Evolving men can have reasonably successful relationships with women assuming they are willing to work and understand what's expected from them.

***Fifth lesson:*** In the FU, women rarely believe the man is fine "as is." They believe there is always room for improvement. The kicker - your willingness to accept that you probably have faults and your willingness to change those things that can be changed will lead to your success in navigating in the FU.

***Sixth lesson:*** In the FU, an evolved man is able to understand that communicating about relationships is important – to the woman.

***Seventh lesson:*** In the FU, women would like their accomplishments to be seen by men with the same exuberance that men expect to receive from women and other men for theirs. Women who want men to help them with household chores should find a way to make it about the man's need for approval and not make it about some emotional need to have the man doing something "for her".

***Eighth lesson:*** In the FU, whatever goes up can come crashing down.

***Ninth lesson:*** In the FU, knowing how to get where you're going is preferable to being told "where to go."

***Tenth lesson***: In the FU, sharing household chores, including grocery shopping is the sign of an evolving male. Asking your partner "first" to share in a pastime activity is a true courtesy. Expecting him or her to share in the activity is just self centered.

***Eleventh lesson:*** In the FU, short and simple only applies to men.

***Twelfth lesson:*** In the FU, food, just like love, is a nurturing tool. Unlike love, too much food can be as bad as too little.

***Thirteenth lesson:*** In the FU, when you get caught not listening just admit that you were deep in thought. When she asks what you were thinking about – simply offer, "I was thinking about you." As for the Vision issue – try not to step in the spilled milk, it will reduce the appearance of your deficiency.

***Fourteenth lesson:*** In the FU, "compromise" usually means that the woman wins!

***Fifteenth lesson:*** In the FU, give a man a fish and he will eat for a day; teach a man to fish and he will have a new way to totally anger his female partner.

www.ingramcontent.com/pod-product-compliance
Lightning Source LLC
Chambersburg PA
CBHW031357040426
42444CB00005B/331